KINDS OF GRACE

Poems

Jennifer Maritza McCauley

Advance Praise for
Kinds of Grace

The sweeping lyricism of these poems sing like arias through the many woes and wonders of womanhood, race, cultures, and homelands. With resolute emotional authority, *Kinds of Grace* inspirits us to not merely exist, but to thrive with dignity and virtue.

—**Richard Blanco**, Presidential Inaugural Poet, author of *Homeland of My Body*

Jennifer Maritza McCauley's new book of poems *Kinds of Grace* is "huge, hot and shining." This collection is a fearless exploration of that which we cannot always name and that which has been buried and silenced for far too long. Using lyrical language, fresh alliteration and anaphora McCauley explores mental health, ancestral memory and what it means to reconnect to and reclaim "Mami's island" as her own. These poems move like tidal waves at times fast and full other times gentle and soft. As we journey through rivers, oceans, graveyards and meadows we see McCauley trying to make sense of her family's past in order to feel rooted in the present as a "panther-soft" Black woman who is learning how to love (herself and others) and be loved. This poignant and timely collection is an affirmation of modern day Black Latina womanhood in all its complexity, humanity and wholeness. This is a book that sings and sighs, offers us grace and light and a field of flowers that reminds us we are still "Alive alive/Alive."

—**Jasminne Mendez**, author of *Aniana Del Mar Jumps In* and *CITY WITHOUT ALTAR*

These days, I don't read poetry to cry or feel helpless. I read it to feel what it feels, to live it deeply and holler its lines like some proud Caribbean woman. That's why I'll read anything Jennifer Maritza McCauley writes. Her poems will as soon hug you loose as shake you tight, have you popping and wincing in beats, singing all kinds of love before morning's arrived.

—**Anjanette Delgado**, Editor, *Home in Florida: Latinx Writers and the Literature of Uprootedness*

McCauley skillfully incorporates an economy of language with evocative imagery and inspiring storytelling. An empowered, engaging voice. Masterful code switching: honoring Black and Boricua cultures. Never apologizing. McCauley is always comfortable in protest and song. McCauley is a must-read poet and author; a rising star in the literary world.

—**Jose Hernandez Diaz**, author of *The Fire Eater* and *Bad Mexican, Bad American.*

KINDS OF GRACE

FLOWERSONG
PRESS

poetry by

Jennifer Maritza McCauley

FLOWERSONG

FlowerSong Press
Copyright © 2024 by Jennifer Maritza McCauley
ISBN: 978-1-963245-28-8

Published by FlowerSong Press
in the United States of America.
www.flowersongpress.com

Cover Art by Evie Shaffer
Cover Design / Typesetting by Priscilla Celina Suarez
Interior Artwork by Maritza González Cintrón and Carol Ward
Set in Adobe Garamond Pro

No part of this book may be reproduced without
written permission from the Publisher.

All inquiries and permission requests should
be addressed to the Publisher.

NOTICE: SCHOOLS AND BUSINESSES
FlowerSong Press offers copies of this book at quantity discount with bulk purchase for educational, business, or sales promotional use. For information, please email the Publisher at info@flowersongpress.com.

To Abba

table of contents

I.

Past 6

Aren't You Afraid? 7

Retribution 8

Rooting 9

Without Control 10

Because Tigers Won't Change Their Stripes 11

In Daddy's House 13

Descansar 17

Apagón 20

Lost in Montjuïc, After Losing 24

Girl Candela 25

After Psalm 23 26

Baggage 27

Kinds of Grace 28

ForeMothers: Canonization, Recreation, Diaspora 29

Cálida 35

Mami 38

In the Meadow 40

Ancestry 41

II.

Diagnosis 47

Worst Case Scenario 49

Mental Health 50

Night in Fort Pierce 51

Waiting 52

Four Days Before Marriage 53

Ugly 55

Tiny Monster 57

Isolation Room 59

Name 62

Why 64

New Clothes 65

Happy Day 66

I can't see you when you're standing right in front of me 67

Lying 69

Cantante 71

Three Days Before Marriage 72

Wedding Day 74

III.

Ars Poetica 81

On Vacation 82

Dark Woman 84

Voices 85

Love Songs for Oceans 86

Naira Kuzmich 89

Carol Ward 91

Inevitable 94

Publication Acknowledgements 95

Acknowledgements 97

About the Author 98

KINDS OF GRACE

1

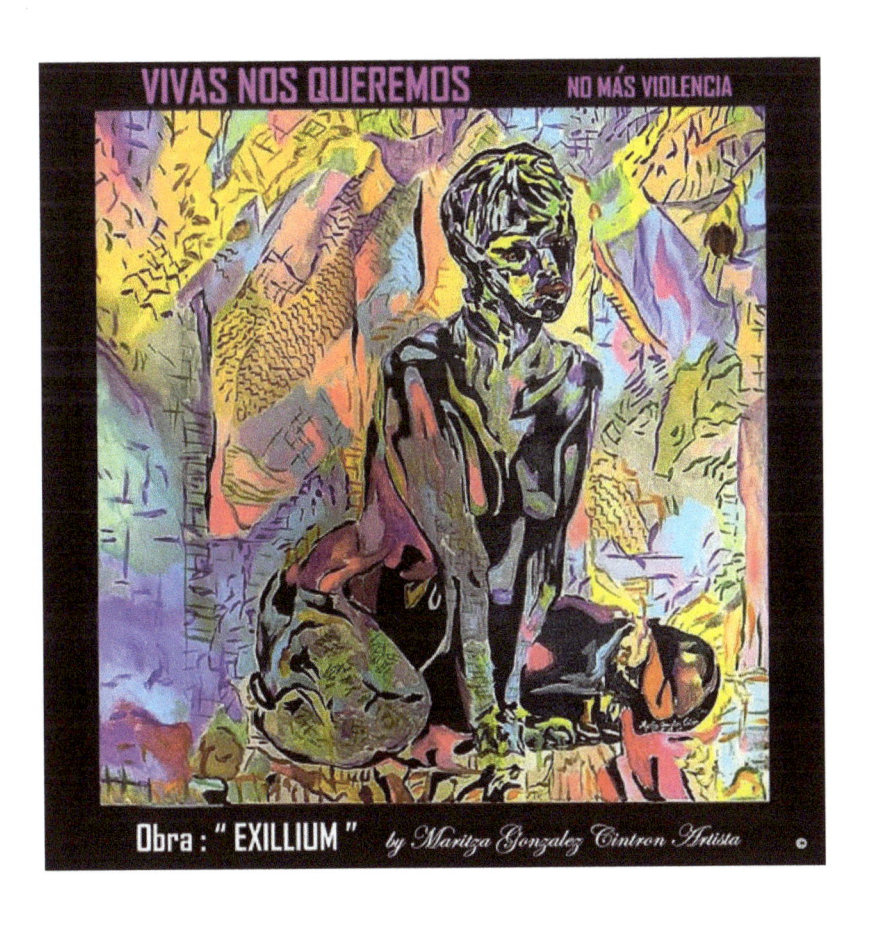

Obra: "EXILLIUM" by Maritza Gonzalez Cintron Artista

Past

I swallow the past, steadying myself against the back of a young birch tree. The past is pulped, palpable; it is large and too-huge to choke down. When I live in the present, I feel newly cleaned and scrubbed by sun. When I face the day brightly, I see the world through baby eyes; I see freckles of color and rainbowed light. So what to do?

What I shall do: I shall defy hauntings. I digest the past, in all its spikes; then I will forget it. I will know the past; it has kissed me blithely and squatted in my house; I will feel the wild grip of past and know it still struggles under my skin but I will not see it. It will be in me, but I will not love it. The past: that ghosted hunger; look, I'm going to ignore my appetite.

Oh present, I open my mouth to consume you in full.

Aren't You Afraid?

If I go down, I'll go down whistling.
Find me border-busting, singing the meanest songs.

I stopped waiting for any new man.

I tramp and burn and tussle.
I soar without stopping.
Your old light dims darker,
But I see perfectly fine.

Yesterday, you asked me, Aren't you afraid?
Of the truck dipped in night, growing closer,
Of the men who ripple the hills, poised to rush down?

I said, I live in motion—I neither rush nor slumber,
Sure, fear is the trickiest insect, but I already
Swatted him down.

Retribution

They told me
I'm not fit to stand near their shoes
And I told them
I'm panther-soft,
I move smoothly,
I sit like swan,
I'm rock-heavy, big as boulder.
They told me I'm the sludge they kick laughing.
I said I'm huge, hot and shining,
I'm the road at midnight without wanderer,
I'm the cool when the night feels like blister.

They told me, told me, told me,
And I stopped listening.

I tell them I'm the rain that drowns sycamores
And births fertile greens. I tell them
Baby, if you can't feel my rain, then
You can't feel a damn thing, and baby

I'm sorry (but not sorry) for you.

Rooting

To root
To stick the firmest parts
Of your body into the heat
Of the earth and see what
Stretches up.

To reach for the lowest
Part of soil and find
Your face there,
Along with the mouths
And minds of misted
Ancestors.
To fit your loving body
Into spaces that know
You fresh.

To seek comfort
In the tongues of flowers.

I am still looking for my best
Ghosts under the grass.

I grow, I grow, I grow.

Without Control

Limitations are a scarcity.
I rise, shaking off the broad shackles of control.
I don't starve next to borders.
I live vibrantly, drenched thick in
Splashing color.
I am not confined to cells or
Shifting undulations.
I walk straight lines easy,
Confirmed in the stride I walk
And you'll see it!
Damn, even if you don't,
I embody the next new
And the dark shallows
I bring into me and shiver off.
Here's the last sorrow:
I don't sense it lasting.
Here's the last pain:
I understand it in full

I love swiftly,
And move soft.
I am here, I decide it;
I am here and I remain
Boldly.

Because Tigers Won't Change Their Stripes

I don't know what to tell you, bro. Sure,

I could water down my nasty,
warm up my shivery, could
sugar-stamp my sour

but I won't.

& I won't switch my skin,
how it spreads on bones
or catches color.

This life is always going to be Black.

Sweet as maví, blazed with
past; nose always going to puff,
hair is always going crinkle into crown

body is always going be grand-sized,

mouth is always going to be picante
before turning
tender.

Daddy always going to have said
fight 'til old roots branch out
blooming, Mami always going to
have cried mucha casera enferma,
get out the damn house and move.

I don't know what the world
will tell me to change today.

How they'll call our cultures
baby-boned, how they'll tell us
we're mewling about corpse problems
who knows how they'll foam and caw.

But I ain't letting their spit
stain this glorious,
not-switching skin.

See: I grow what I should.
Parts that got you shook: Nope.
This mouth is always going to be full-open,
this trap
a Black hole.

This Black life
is always going to be here,
howling so loud sounding
something like

temblor.

In Daddy's House

Don't worry, daughter,
I'll teach you how
to talk.

Don't suck your teeth
for nothing.

Pick your times to tussle,
let your anger be choice.
Babygirl, if you cuss,
make sure that Blackmouth
kills.

On all days,
fit your face tight.
Keep the mouth a strong
line. When sweet folks
come around, do good.
Go silent for those who do
you mean, unless the stink
of injustice gets too foggy,
fat or foul, if it gets
'til you can't smell a thing
but sin, then, daughter,
you tussle.

On normal days, stay even.
Toughen the eyes.
No slippage from the
eye-ducts, forget all your crooked,
leaking scars.

Remember the price of showing
hurt, so: choose your hurt.
Rarely show them your hurt-twisted face.
So then: Smile. Nod
twice. Get ready.

Remember your woman-body.
Remember your damn
skin.

And if life gets too nasty,
if you can't remember
how to act cool, girl,
imagine your insides
are a long blue sky
flustered with happy cloud.
Imagine your arms are flapping
and you're flying soft,
tell yourself you're
coasting.

Imagine the wind
is sugar-tasting and sounds
like me or your Mami singing
love, imagine you are floating
in that little inside-place that is

only owned by you. Stay in that
inside-place while all the rest are
screaming.

Stay there, thinking about blue, even
while folks snatch your shoulders,
shake you back to pain, you stay
there, even if your whole life
is screaming.

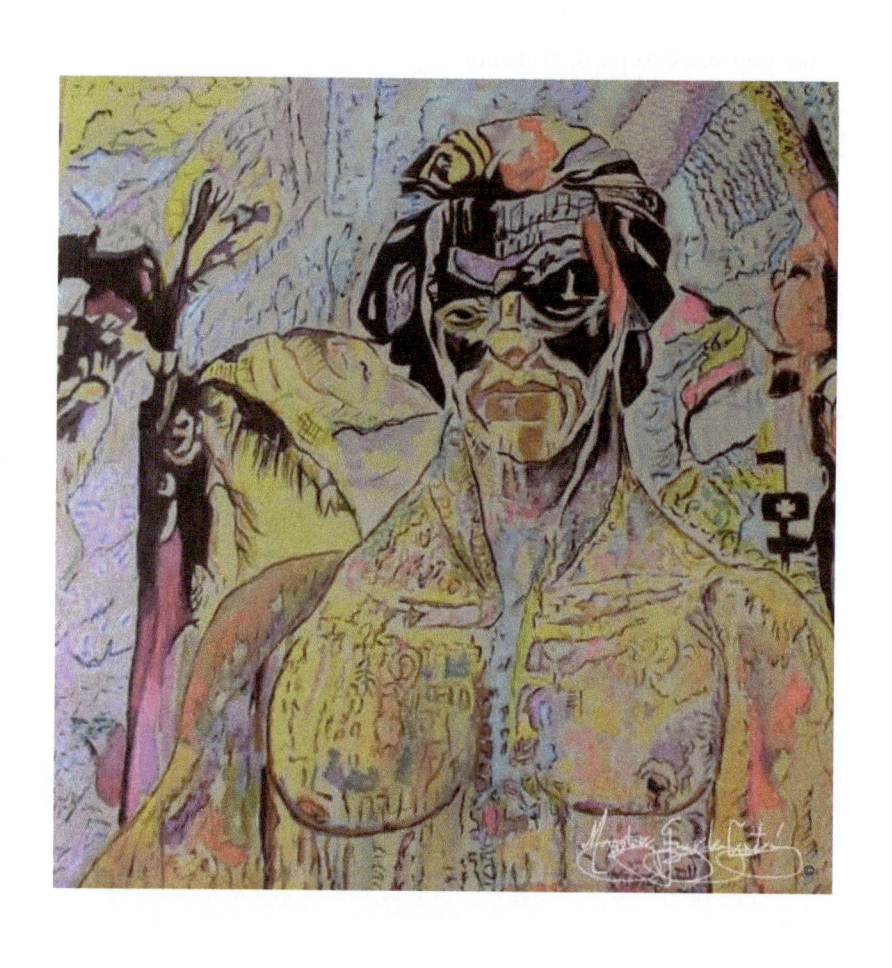

"Agüeybaná"
by Maritza González Cintrón

Descansar

treefrogs titter in the campo, mirrorwater
shrugs sweet behind Joyuda's docks
ocean scrunches the stress and secrets de las olas

waves pinken under sunset's passing
flor de magas crown snoozing ceiba
isla is wet, thick, and ancient
stilted casas in mami's pueblo sleep calm.

you are here too, you: family and safe spot
I carry with me in unrooted spaces.
we drink medalla on the porch with full tribe,
they see me distracted and say in Spanish,

"why don't you see where we are
as real, not imaginary?"
and I say "tengo que, tengo que—"
and forget descansar when I was looking for it
what'sthewordpalabrapalabrapalabra

an easy one. I say sorry to mami's island, everyone,
I say, my tongue is not your tongue, and they say
you forget the word
because you don't know how
to rest.

tonight, my family sleeps under thin sheets
and I am watching you rest in Cabo Rojo
as I have for so long, sly nose half-pressed to pillow.
after years of losing, your return was slow,
not fuego but measure, crest curling before
plunge, breeze stroking pleats of home-water.

when I forget first loves and languages,
come to confusion and culture again,
real love falls huge and quiet,
like the blanket you give me when I tell you my
feet are cold in the summer, while
the coquis chatter through the walls,
singing like mami did when I was a child
descansa, descansa, my girl
just rest.

"Continuamos"
by Maritza González Cintrón

Apagón

For those lost in Hurricane Maria

Tonight, after the blackout on Mami's native
island, there is no sleep on my side of American
country. Instead, there is Mami's isla del encanto, smeared
across my black eyes, there is the wail of coqui lungs,
the yellow writhe of yuca snapped in half, the wet crack
of palmtrunk kicked across La Perla by history-old wind,
the toss of green-glow'd bay in Fajardo, the raise of graffit'd brick,
the empty stages of El Bori, where mi prima y yo
danced to buleadores pounding drumskin
pa'la playa, pa' la calle, for unshackled spirits.

Tonight, I think about my mother's island,
heavy with the weight of mainland,
which shares the colors of the Boricua flag,
the red-blue-white
we are so proud to ink on our breasts,
to stitch on our stomachs,
because we make these colors
fit our brown skin right.

I think about Mayagüez on Memorial Day,
empty, save for a joint that played Coldplay
and Hector. Mayagüez, where Cristobal's statue stood
in the Plaza, his shoulders high and smug, hands

outstretched like faux Cristo, the lady slaves
and Tainas, these estatuas behind him, limply clutching
torches, staring away.

I think about when I dipped feet in purple Ponce water,
the happy vendedor who threaded a bracelet made of
coral, conch, and twine on my wrist,
tight enough so it wouldn't come off.
I think of the viejito who kissed both of my cheeks last June
and said: No existe un corazon Americano. Tienes sangre negra,
Taina, blanca. In the States and here,
you are Boricua.

Tonight, my Mami calls me from her American city,
says she is thinking of our island, and wonders
with tiny tongue, what is left,
where are our people.

We ask each other these questions,
and do not have answers.
We whisper in lighted rooms in American cities,
as if the ghosts of our family-gods
can hear our fear.
A week later, we talk loudly of pain, of the pueblo
ravaged, my mother's birthplace. We talk with family
from her town, about political slapbacks,
our friends who cannot access food
or life-basics. We talk all day to our family, and turn
on the TV to see a line in front of the
blue-white-red lights of a Ponce Walmart.
We think of who is hurt, where are our gente,
what has not been done.

But, tonight, in a Boricua blackout,
I wonder who is running
past dark shores
on my mother's island?
I wonder what jibaro is stamping across campo alone?
Who is dancing bomba in white dress?

We know somebody is dancing.
We know some countryman is climbing along.

We wonder who is dying.

We know
somebody,
on our island,
is
dying.

"Nostalgia" — Maritza Gonzalez Cintron

Lost in Montjuic, After Losing

When you loved a body and lost it easy
you'll see the damn thing
everywhere, in every soft-smiled face or
seraph-ed city sculpture but

                        look

That body lost you too, after its heel-spin
away see:

what is left is not that body

because that body that mattered
is not anywhere,
not in clear coffin box, not in loamy earth
not wherever it is now, perhaps alive, shunning,
forgetting you

Now, that body is your funerary art,
ever-mattering, nowhere, amaranthine,

it is your trail
outside of the mausoleum.

The body is not anywhere,
and you are   left,

looking.

Girl Candela

How to be bold as a spirit? Not ruled
By bordering eye, polyphias of projection.

There are advantages to invisibility. The Elders say:
Living is more about how you manage your life.

Still, I envy the gone and sainted, so free-speaking,
So daring in immortality, ancestral fount.

How many flores grow in the teeth of the living?
They asked me to speak at a girl's funeral.

I did, for her honor, but couldn't edit my explanations;
I failed to capture her. She looked too much like me.

Running wasn't right either, so I sang insufficient hymn.
At the lip of grave: her voice turned mirror, the mirror to ghost.

That ghost turned to spirit, and the spirit, prayer.
Here are the glories of being loud without yelling, to incant

without a mourning mouth. To call for help
and see the sources of all normal Saints, candela-bright.

Here is a dream that you too, unfinished,
                         (even today)

could feel as innocent

                                      as a completed life.

After Psalm 23

So what, pray/tell, do you want?
    After pastures don't green better?
    After the shaggiest wool is shorn?
I told you plenty of times, before you wept
yourself to heart-slaughter:

Water the forb first. Chill out.
Don't waste time thinking about blood or meat.
No need to shiver, bone-shown, to strangers. Let shepherds lead.
    You're not an overflowing cup, but a fleshy you.
                Lay down on your mat, at times, tire.
I'm trying to help you, little self, while you resist
    me, mid-tremble.
Dead in the valley of the shadow of death
    You are not who you have always been---
Good. Reborn wild in still waters; kid, you're fine.
    Surely, mercy is a goodness, surely mercy is your right.

Baggage

On the new lawn,
rhododendron petals
wilt in a blue
jay's mouth.

A sign, I think. Some kind of glory?

I get closer: No petals.
The jay just caught toilet paper
in her beak.

There she goes:
just dragging that shit along.

I wonder how many
flowers I think live in my teeth,
when they're just dead nothings
I carry around.

                      (But they're mine!)

Kinds of Grace

Beach-bidden, I see
bulges of sand and conch chunk,

banked coral, halved shells, hard
like fingernail face. Bounce of Wellcraft,

air-sprint of searching pelican.
Prasine wave, pleat of ocean ripple,

loose unbind of fulling tide.
A break of wave, another break.

Today, special and ordinary, a crowd
has formed under blazing blue.

Baby shark lies ashore, twitching.
A family reeled her in after fishing, thought

she was a large cobia, not a small blacktip.
Throw it back! Some say, others say, *eat*!

While the crowd debates, a tide rolls in,
cradles the baby's body. Like grace,

the sea carries her back home.

ForeMothers: Canonization, Recreation, Diaspora

Canonization of Foremothers

Who is that mother starving next to the alphabet?
Promise: she ate every letter clean and whole.

We are her daughters, glowing healthy
From her graphemes. Bloated, brainy chicks in her nest.

She feeds us scriptures and griot fires,
Serves cooked-well auguries, and says go forth

She looks hungry to you, but we see her constant
Feasting, her hands clawing for what she wants

What she must pass down.

Recreation

Bought my arms from a tienda en Ponce, face
From Daddy's House of Immovable masks,
Got the figure from a Miami mannequin, made
The mouth from hawthorn and yucca hair.

Hocked my knees from some sycamore upriver,
Snatched the toes from a coltsfoot downstream.
Caught the walking from a Saturday straggler.
Got the float from a seraph riding the 87 Morningside

Breaststroke came from Yemaya, after she kicked off.
The baladas grew from Mami, who said *óyeme*:

After you leave me: recreate yourself
As you will.

Plant, sky, branch, anthem, girl:
When you choose your final parts:

You better at least keep singing

my damn songs

Diaspora

For an afternoon, Georgie offered me friendship and $50 dollars' worth of Kanekalon jumbo, included in the box style. Braiding hair, silk-soft and crimped, blackest at the tips. I took her offers, because I wanted a friend and saved enough money to buy a new version of myself that month.

Georgie's salon was in the living room of her apartment in Fort Monroe; she lived alone. She looked like me, Black and huge-eyed, except she was better—taller and glowing; all her glowing was blindingly unachievable. She clicked her tongue when she dipped her hands into my massive hair, told me I let my coils tangle too-badly. Her oiled fingers worked my knots until they sprung loose. When she unraveled the clumps to lanky root, she said, "This isn't all bad. But you've got to take care of what you own, what is attached to you."

She washed the life-gunk from my curls, then washed again, air-dried it, combed it out. With a comb tip, she divided the hair into four squares that looked like quilt-blocks. To hold the braid, she weaved in that Kanekalon, the sort that fit my texture different, reminding me nothing fake will truly fit. Georgie braided the three strands, *one-two-three, one-two-three*. I felt all this looping and threading and overlapping but couldn't see the job being done. Her work was fast and sharp, but my head, in all its red throbbing, felt all right, like it was loosing itself from something. With every finished braid, with every thin river of scalp exposed, there was roughness, then relief. This pull and twist, under Georgie's hands, felt necessary, like passed-down power. When Georgie saw me wince, she told the back of my head, "This is your process. Just how it goes."

Georgie kept going, and my chair got hot from Virginia sunrays slamming through the window. Her phone was ringing, and she ignored it. She asked me about my life, and I told her it was small, Black and normal, now. That I lived on many islands, lost my lovers during several squalls, but I knew how to survive. I told her I'd taken well to living alone. She said, "That's the way it goes, how it goes," and we traded platitudes, angrily,— que sera sera, life goes on and on and on and—-. She saw me wriggling and said, "Hold still. I'm taking care of you. So you can do this yourself," and I obeyed.

I asked Georgie how she got her name. She didn't tell me, but she did tell me about the man called George who stamped his name upon her. This George ripped my stylist from her green home when she was full-bodied and middle-aged. He wanted her Guinea grains and golds, her sparkling sugars and breadfruits stuffed hot inside of her womb. This George pretended to love her, because he saw how fresh her body was, smelling like damp sand and dewdrops. He decided he wanted to take what she had, nibble on her slow so he plotted how best to snatch her lovely things. One night, George gave her a mixed potion that knocked her out. He took her body into his own, beat her bad, threw her over his shoulder and swum back to his home with my stylist on his back. He beat her again, then left her to work on his fields. She lived foul, unwillingly committed to the amber lands he'd stolen from another dark woman. My stylist was called wild and unseemly, so like something wild, she bounded from George on another night, she made her own kind of free.

As she told her story, she twisted the three parts of my hair, the plastic myths, the ancestral truths, the unknotted real. She intertwined these strands like she was stitching something into me. I asked her if she thought about George because she had his name, and she said he didn't matter. She told me George tried to find her, years later, in the wilderness, but he couldn't, and she lived with others like her. They all hid and fled, hid and fled, and grew older. Years after she'd found a little place to live, liberated, and George showed up and he'd grown enormously in size. He'd gobbled up lots of names, her original one too, that's why he was so large and tall. He stood in her door and she looked him in the eye while he watched her. Her looking made him mad and he left, promising to bring an army for her, and she said: *try*. She missed all the parts he took, felt pissed about how big he'd become, but she decided he could never take anything because he was nobody. She could steal his name back, she could become anyone, and still be herself. So she rebirthed herself, and lived all of her lives, looking forward.

I didn't know what to say. Her body was fresh-smelling and

seemed to hold every secret I wanted to know. I was afraid for her, because I knew why someone would hunt her down; she had infinite riches. I asked if her original name was Motherland, or the name of another pillaged country and she said, "Yes. If you see it that way, all those names are mine."

She kept braiding, the twisting got tighter, it hurt more and I didn't know if I wanted to have these braids in anymore because this all hurt so bad, the yanking and tugging, and I wanted to scream or tell her to stop, but I bit my tongue so she could see I was as strong as her real, dark hair. My teeth sunk into my tongue too-deep, and I tasted blood and realized I'd never tasted my own blood; it was sea-salty and foreign and confusing. The pain in my head and mouth got worse, the braids came together even quicker now. She asked me my name, what I was called, and I couldn't remember.

Georgie said she was willing to share her life now, with any girl or daughter, after what had happened. She told me she knew me before I was born, that I was from a green home too. I told her about my islands, my parents whose faces I'd forgotten long ago. I told her about my time with pirates and schemers and merchants, who had stolen things from my womb too. I told her I missed my parents. I told her I didn't know how to change; I was used to being unrooted. She said, "That's a privilege. Choosing when to change. Hold still, Daughter Diaspora. Wait, now, right there—-" Hours later she finished my hair. The hours didn't feel that long. They merely stretched on indefinitely into past and future, like a song without a final downbeat. When Georgie was done with my hair, she stepped back and looked at me. She turned me around in the chair and showed me my face in the mirror. The braids looked good, they stretched down my body to my ass, my scalp was exposed for the world to take a peek. I thought I looked lovely and out of place. I shook the heavy hair, didn't know how it should feel, all I knew is that it felt heavy.

"By the way," she said to the mirror. "My name's not Georgie. Not George. Never was. Someone just told you that and you believed it. Here, in this…" She patted my tough, finished braids. "I've sewn a map that goes wherever you go." Then she told me her real name, and I tasted the leftover blood in my mouth. She said her name again, and then mine, and I wept in her apartment, because both names sounded so beautiful together. I'd never heard them before, and I felt pit-deep shame. I told her I was sorry, sorry, for thinking we could be called anything else, that we could make sense in any other tongue but the unspeakable.… She stepped away from me, kept one hand on my shoulder. I gave her two one hundred dollar bills, Ben-face down, and she waved it away like this was the wrong time. She looked at our reflection in the glass and kissed me on the forehead.

We looked back in the mirror, and saw ourselves loving our whole heads. We glowed then; we are glowing still.

Cálida

I.
When I was a babygirl Mami took me
to all the malls and she hated watching
the twig-thin moms with the trunk-thick kids
manacled by Velcro leashes and she said:
*this is the way Americans are with their babies,
I would never shackle my child to me.*

One day, Mami took me to
one of the malls because she wanted to buy
me one of those little jackets that keep babies
warm and Mami kneeled down in the OshMcGosh
section and said to me: *stayatmyhip there are people who
snatch little children like you.*
She said: *stay near me while I shop for your new jacket,
I need to keep my baby warm.*

Mami took too-long looking for the
coats that keep babies warm. She thought
all the fabrics were flimsy and the down was
poorly made and she was afraid the sleeves might
break apart in the snow and I'd freeze
to death on the way to the school where the
whitekids were foul. While she got mad at the coats
I decided I would wander off, because I
was not like the kids on Velcro leashes, I was free,

selfish and bored with all of Mami's endless
caring.

I called out: I'm leaving, heyhey, I'll
be off and she didn't hear me.
When Mami turned I left anyway because
there were shiny and interesting things beyond her
and the boys on leashes looked funny and fun so
I ran through all of the kid-dresses on little
girl legs, and there I was, a Blackbaby unbound
in an American mall.

Quickly, I got lost and I was somewhere amongst
scowling lady-faces and the kids on leashes who
tried to run a circle around their mothers to trip them,
and they ran a circle around me and I tripped
somewhere in the Big Ladies department
next to the Big Men suits.
I called out for Mami, somewhere in an American mall,
amongst parents who didn't laugh and children
who were always asking for something huge.
A longtime later Mami appeared, red-faced,
weeping, with a stuffed bag of
tiny coats and she said:
Why would you leave me, hija, I'm trying to
keep you warm and safe?

I cried baby-tears and thought with
a baby-mind: this is how I hurt love:
by running off
and this is how love is proven:
when your mother goes looking for you
after you've left her to mourn

your absence

and she finds you,
always, always.

II.
in some relationships,
men get mad
at my confusing spirit
and say things like:
maybe the only person
who will ever love you
right is your mother.

Mami

When I hear the strum of Latin music,
the heart-heat of a cantante
Crooning for women tucked
Deep into shuddering strings
Your face, Mami, bursts forth, gleaming

When the Guayanilla sea coughs up frills
Of foam and I hear the twirl
And twist of Spanish as the coquis weep,
Mami, you come

When I'm in a bar and the man
Next to me says Soy Boricua and he shows me
The tattoos of the flag stitched into his skin
I feel the fast surge of kinship
And your face arrives

This identity, yours, brims
And burns and fills me
Sweetly
I can't speak your language
Without your mouth
I can't walk through crowds
Without you hovering

Here we are now, as we are
In our union, hearing each other's voices,
You remain, pa'siempre

In the Meadow

Dear Mami,
    Let's go to the meadow
    Let's start anew
    Amid wind-nudged reeds
    And flapping floras
    Let's gobble up the smear
    Of sky, let's run to the lake
    And swim in its wrinkled
    Blue face

    Let's call to the catbirds
    Our voices heaving and wild
    Let's sing to the drifting doe
    Let's love the jumping cardinal

    Let's run to the oaken cabin
    It's small and perfect for love
    Let's live anew in that place,
    You'll cook sometimes, I will too

    We'll trade secrets in wooden walls
    You'll smile often, I will too.

Dear Mami,
    Let's go to the meadow
    Let's finally exhale.

Ancestry

Again, I'm whipped with whisps of bloodroots.

I carry my family gods on these new shoulders,
Their rivers sit on my thick back. When I think
Of these old ones, I become a stranger, I keep
Forgetting my full name.

Their bodies hurried through calling water.
They fled states, cut through star-split
nights and bleak rivers, with no
Thirst nor slake. They came to freedom hurt
And wilting, but still they came.

In museums, they return,
Their names in books I read for the first time.

On the way home years ago, I passed
A graveyard of the Missouri enslaved
They were buried underneath unmarked stone,
Their graves sat behind the headstone of a white man
A statue of an angel was dedicated to him.
The graveyard is historical, my father's homestate says.
That white man's face
Is on a polished plaque. He is smiling.

Stunning history, refreshing on pages and screens,
The dead still lay, so many names unknown.

I carry the load I did not carry and I am here in person,
For no reason but to sing the dead's old songs.

"Alma Libre"
by Maritza González Cintrón

2

Diagnosis

I am cooking and I get the diagnosis
On the telephone and after I finish
Talking to the mental health nurse I call my mother
and she says what are you cooking
and I tell her Nothing-It's-Terrible. I tell her
I'm trying to make arroz
Con gandules, but I'm not making the
Beans right, not like you do and she
Asks me what I'm doing wrong
And I tell her everything and that
It's clear I'm a mess, I'm a big mess
Thick with penink and tangles of thought
That keep twisting fierce and if there's a knob
Of lighted clarity in all that chaos, who knows,
If you could see my mind Mami, you'd see that
It's a train that never stops mowing forward
And on the worst nights I imagined myself
Jumping in front of its charge but now the
Nurse says if I listen and obey I can train-hop
And survive.

My mother asks what I'm talking about
And I ask her why I keep burning the rice,
and she gives me the instructions to make
gandules proper, don't get ahead of yourself
she says, use pepper and sazón, just enough

tomato sauce, wait
Until the sauce bubbles. I ask her why
I keep burning the rice, is it because every mistake
I make is an extension of the mistake inside of me
and she says, girl, the burned rice
bottom is called pegao,

She says many would say the pegao
is the best part.

When I eat my food later, I think she
Is right, it tastes just fine.

Worst Case Scenario

I've mourned my life before I've died
It's pitiful, but that's the way I go about it.

I imagine the car crushed before it drives
I see the plane mid-crash before it soars.
I curse you for leaving before you've arrived.

What to do with these imaginings?
It's easy to see how I'd tumble into fall
What to do with this grim thinking?
Without effort, I can't grow into love

To cure the mind, I think of a field
Reckless in its immobility and waving flora
I smell sun tucked under unwintered blossoms
I imagine only that field until disaster fades

Mental Health

On a new afternoon, I awake
And the mass wakes with me.

I can't see it but it's large.
I can't see it but it's fond of gooey gab
I can't see it but it's boulder-heavy,
I can't see it but I know I can't get around
it's damning size.

It squats on my chest and takes a shit.
It squats on my back and twerks into me
It squats on my head and its ass is on my eyes

This mass has no love for me, that's certainly true.

On a cold afternoon, I awake
And greet the mass.
It says fuck you and I go about my business.

I tuck the mass in deep so I can't see its shape
I tuck the mass in my bloodstream and hope it dies

On a different night, I forget the mass exists.
This is how I go about these days:
Battling for the next moment, knowing
I don't care if the mass is crushing my neck
Or if it ever existed at all.

Night in Fort Pierce

The night has a pretty good attitude
Star-stripped and rushing,
I imagine a librettist
Singing complexities to the
Black-blue spread above.

The sand is flat and vague-looking.
The ocean is roaring fierce.
The pelicans squat, huddle and rest.
Cars complain softly.

It's so quiet it's cacophonous
The night says I've got this fine.

I can't sleep but I absorb
The black air's chattering.

I can't sleep but the wind
Cradles me alive.

Waiting

I'm not ripe for mating, So I carry myself well.

Underscored jaw,
Neck like lazy swan.
                (I'm joking. Not swan: jaunting cockatiel.)

I'm not really sure how you do it. Just being you: which interminably is resplendent.

I know I've got it too: The beat and fast hips, the wait and hide. I know the rituals to catch you:

And they bore me; you don't bore me.
Now here you are, laughing about some normal thing.

Here I go, gone. I bid you good luck. I love you alone, now, then a bit later, in my room

                Where you can't see the extent.

Four Days Before Marriage

I sink into a familiar space
Fizz of new drink, wild thoughts next

It's another night
I'm talking to people I don't know.

A widowed man's speaking about his wife
When I tell him I'm getting married on Friday
He talks about a woman who was a "living angel"
He shows me her picture
She's afire, blonde, with a cheering smile

She "put up with me" he says
and I think of how you put up with me

You know the kitchen knives in my brain,
The black nights I've spent screaming
You know the floor grabs,
The tumbles and how the diagnosis
Tells me it's over but the me inside of me
Tells me I'm still alive

He's telling me how she always knew his ways
And I think how you always know the direction
I'll stray, you know where I'll run when I disappear
You know how to retrieve me

You know the claws for Black-brown identity, the times
I said, can anyone understand my childhood
You said the only words I need to hear
Which are "I'm with you" and fuck, you're always with me

I cry when he talks about his dead wife because I think
Of you, very much living, in our home, cooking dinner
Waiting for me to come home.

Ugly

The first thing the white girl said was "you're too dirty to be touched" because I was Black-skinned, dark as a copper penny. She says my skin is shit brown, it was the color of shit, you are doo doo, she says, and I don't know what to do with that so I let it go. This is the familiar process when you are a Black child in an all-white school, you let it go, let it go, let it go, let it go, let it go, let it go , let it go

Let it

Fucking

                        Go.

She says she won't touch my Polly Pockets because she's afraid the black will rub off on her and she'll be Black like me and nobody will like her because she's too Black too Black too too Black too Black

Too BLACK

In a description of myself to my friends in college I take her words back and say I am too fucking Black. Hell yeah, I am too BLACK.

Years later she tells me she thinks Black men don't like Black girls, that they only like white girls like her. She comes up to me and says this and every time I love a Black man I think of her face.

When we were children, she drew a picture of a beautiful princess with golden hair and she came up to me and said this is me, I'm beautiful and in a rage I couldn't think because I thought of everything she'd said to me so I told her you can't be that princess you are UGLY and her mouth fell open and I still feel guilty about telling her this twenty nine years later and I don't know what this says about me so I let this

All

Go

I just let it go

Let it go

Let it go

Let it go

Let it fucking

Go

Tiny Monster

My dinner shrinks
The room becomes
A roaming kind of violence
Graven ashes stir in the fireplace

I am sitting in the chair
And I feel like falling, my head
Is shocking me into quiet

You're talking but I can't hear you
Your voice is a bird, balded
And trying for flight

I want to get up but my legs
Are still and rock-laden

I think, *I am having a panic attack*
And the words thrust into me
and catch my tongue, wrench it out
and I tell you what's happening
and you're getting up

Your hands are a bullet as they grip me
I recoil and try to run
I talk to the tiny monster that's raging
And pitiful behind my ribcage

Your arms are around me and I fight back
You arms are talking about love and
Your whispers are a chilling balm

Before I pass out, I think about your
Face, shining like a spotlight

Isolation Room

When doing EMDR,
The therapist tells you to go back
To the Isolation Room,
The place in the psychiatric ward
Where you have become too wild-mouthed and beastly
To be loved like a warm, laughing human,
when you must
sit on a prison bed and think
About your own Black face without window
Or neighboring flesh.

You remember this place, how
You sat on the prison bed and wailed loud
How you discovered that you had the ability
To bargain fierce, that you'd give up your life if you could see
 the flash of another wriggling body, if you could feel
untethered air blasting from the punched-in A/C.

You remember how you banged on the door and hollered
I'll do anything, anything, just let me out.

At that point you would do it,
Anything. Whatever they asked,
No matter how terrible, you didn't
Want to be Animal, you didn't want
To be left alone, confined to your own skin

You'd bet your life on an eyelash-length
Of hope and in that blackening place
you slapped the floor hard, there
You found it: the rock bottom.

You were once a person who would read
Poems on long stages to audiences smothered with love
Who studied Derrida and Morrison
In PhD classes and damn it you earned that
Doctorate but you still ended up here.

You were in your own clothes at least,
So you clutched them to your breast
And told yourself, at least I have this,
My own shirt and my own breath that
Winds and fumes out of my tired lips and reminds
Me, *I have this life, I have this life*, and look here,
I'm alone but *I'm still huffing*
And puffing like angel, look here: I'm still alive.

The therapist wants you to go back to this place,
And when you do you, your head fills with maelstrom and you
Can't see her face on Zoom.
You wilt and you hear her saying
Come back to me, come on, come back.

When you return, you see the reality:
That you are yourself in your own clothes
That you picked yourself, and she is as she is
Staring at you, wondering about the next moment.

You realize you are exactly where you were
In the Isolation Room, breathing big in your own Black skin
You are the same as you were back then,
Alive alive

Alive.

Name

I didn't come out of the womb knowing my name
But I have it stitched like peeling scar on my body
and damn it I take it in me as my own

The first name, full-throated and multi-syllabic
The second Puerto Rican, stamped on me after
My prima who paints bursting flowers and swelling shores

Rosa Parks' maiden name is my last one
It's stone-heavy with whiteness and ownership
But That Special Woman shares it too
So this last name I claim as my own,
in my Blackness

I am a Black woman stomping
And stepping in this name
I am a Puerto Rican woman salsa-shimmying
in this name

I shout soliloquies in this name, I weep laments
in this name,
I tear my hair out in this name and I
Come back from the aging depths
In this name.

This name is made of bubbling slave blood
This name is made of Guayanilla coqui-skin
And chitlins

This name sounds like a sweet dirge on a Sunday morning
This name hollers like the scream you can't keep in

I am this name and I don't give a damn if you remember it.

Look here
I write the words that come to me softly,
in the violet night air and I'll whisper love to you
In the song my mother gave me as a child, and
That's how I'll go about this life
In this name.

Why

When your skull empties
And you look at the spiky baubles
And new blues strewn on your old floor
You have realized you are
Clean-feeling, refreshing
Refreshing. You barely
Recognize the you that has
Washed and bled out
Your watery ghosts

And now comes the tricky part
Why: the stickiest question
After the foam has dried

The question that chills and pins

What was the point of this all?
The nights body-flat on
Wooly carpets
The nights spent without salve
Why would this all happen?

The answer is stuck in the breast
It's emerging but not fully formed
It's living but not alive

You wait on it, for now, it's fine
To just to wait

New Clothes

I try on fresh garb
Clothes like blazing light I've picked for myself
Swishing dresses I wear for the first time.
I buy the perfect fit.

I stride and prance and prowl
It's a fun thing to fashion an adorned you

I tell you all this and you're laughing
You wear your Grandma's polos, I wear floral print
You agree you like the sensation
Of finding yourself anew in a pressed shirt

Here I am waltzing into another Tuesday
Here I am teaching a class, feeling fine
Here I am in my new outfit asking questions
And thinking my thoughts can't be all that terrible
As long as I concentrate on the faces in front of me
And feel the brush of fabric on my legs

It takes something as small as a skirt
I find on sale to remind me
I can feel real If I'd like to

Happy Day

What if I spent the day with face blasted
By shine, with sparks alighting the
Long parts of my aging face

What if I spent the day in stride with you
Never wondering if you'd see me, I'd just be
affixed to your God-smeared eyes

What a day that would be
I wouldn't wonder about scarcity or want
Failure or low feeling

What if the day was, as it is,
Brightly skinless and naked
Drenched in swallowing yellow?

That would be great.
Let's do it this way.
Here, your fingers can become
My fingers and we'll walk
Like this, intertwined, perhaps
Skipping like children

Let's see this out as it should be
Today we will be sopping
With light

I can't see you when you're standing right in front of me

I talk to you all the time. I become you when you speak to me in words I understand.

I am you because we are bound now but because of that tight bind baby I can't see you properly. you're so much in me I am forgetting our boundaries and here I'll try to reason with you and you are me, listening to   you   you you   you are

My   projection

You say projection in therapy-words like it's a bad thing but baby I'm just telling you and everyone that I call "you" that *I see you everywhere and in every small thing* and when I see you I see myself wandering through fields of filtered light and when I come out of the flashing there is you and you are me and

we are together whenever I see myself in you

Sometimes I look for you and you don't appear. Sometimes I scream for you and you return. Sometimes you're so close all I can see is your pores and I can't remember if you liked your chicken braised or boiled.

Sometimes you tell me my name and all I hear is yours and then I tell you my name and you become me.

I can't see you when you're standing right in front of me.

But I can see the hairs on your neck rise and I can smell the oil on your face-skin.

You are reading my words now and now you are in me.

Maybe we'll remain this close, maybe we are supposed to be this intimate.

I don't know.

Let me know later, oh beautiful you.

I can't see you when you're standing right in front of me.

Lying

It's time for the ultrasound
And the technician seeks
To check my heart.

I'm tied up to ribboning wire,
Gelled electrodes grasp my
Chest-skin.

Do you have anxiety? Or something else?
He asks immediately
As his eyes roam the screen,
Yes, I tell him. I do. And Something Else.

I'm surprised he can tell,
I thought I was able to mask
it, stuff it fiercely inside until faux
calm slips out.

Apparently my heart doesn't lie.

You get up from your chair
And stroke me gently,

Keep doing that, the technician
Tells you. *Yes, that's right
Now her heart rate is perfect.*

I sink into your nested warmth,
Your fingertips
Speak baby
lullabies to my twisted arm.

Tender you, you give me
sacred rest, with you
Fears and sorrow are sliced down
To slivers of nothing.

Apparently, my heart doesn't lie.

Cantante

This warm mouth of the city bleats
The Houston night limps over
And hangs on the high moon.

The cantante is singing about
Lonely doves and his guitar speaks
About dead love and bathroom stalls
And forward motion.

I am sitting here, an eye
Ingesting the full body of the dark.
I am loving the funk and jive of the
Cheering people

I am here, forgetting about flashing
Screens and the call of earthen graves.

The cantante cries about sun and
I see its face, aching with light.

Music can wash you, jig you alive
In the spring of the moment.

On this night, the cantante
Thrills me to wake.

Three Days Before Marriage

Our families are bustling and broad-mouthed
Percolating stories spreading
I am listening, listening
You are talking too; you know everyone
close

My family can fit in the palm of my hand
Just my father, my mother, my brother
And me
We cleave to your growing tribe
We speak as we should, easily

What to tell you about my few people
We are our own drifting island

What to tell you about how I grew up?
That these were the only people I loved?
You have so many attachments in your life
But these are my golden three

Even if you don't understand
I want you to see them:

My father: full-Afro'd and chatting glibly
My mother: spreading hands and laughing wild
My brother: big-voiced and grinning like lightbeam

I want you to see them in their glory
I want you to see me when you see
Their faces

My dark people, reaching for the ceiling
That's ever distancing itself from us

Wedding Day

God knew your needs when He brought you together. He knew exactly what you needed to make you complete.
—Jan Leonard

Violet flora buds, fragrant-fumed
Ivory linens, hanging lush
Dress, sequined and flowing huge
Bodice restricting breath

I think of you when I get ready
The time before I see you brazenly
stretches on
After I am done
they tell me to look to the window

When I see you then I can walk
I'm in the space without you, yearning
When I am most nervous I clutch your hand
But you aren't here, when I am most afraid

Before they took me to the mental hospital
They snatched you from me too, I think of that time again

When they say my name, I'm startled
Weak-kneed ,they lead me to my parents
Who wait with upturned mouths

My song comes on and I'm walking
Parents steady me, I'm moving strong
I see you, you're not too far off
When I reach you, your eyes are soft and trembling
When I see you I sob

As the officiant talks, you fill my vision
Normal-mouthed, eyes glinting sweetly
You are you and fear bursts easily
When I'm with you everything becomes
Free-feeling and comfortable, you are not just husband
You are limb, finger, toe, snapped rib

When the officiant asks me to repeat
After her, there's you
When I make my vow, there's you
In the morning, with fuming coffee poured
There's you
In the evening, when chilly wine clinks
There you are

Here in this moment, I see you
As if I'd known you since birth
And here in this moment
I say the officiant's words
As if they are my own

Do you promise to love him, comfort him, honor and keep him, in sickness and in health, and forsaking all others, remain faithful to him as long as you both shall live?

I do. I do. I do. I-

I promise to find you if you sprint off searching
I promise to tuck you in when the air quiets quick
I promise to kiss you to sleep when the nights come screeching
I promise to stand by your bedside when you can't rise
I promise to call you to talk about penumbras
I promise to keep you safe if trouble comes calling fierce
I promise to love you with full, aching love until death splits us
I promise I'll call you mine until my lips can't wriggle or move

I promise to love you because you
Will always be the most
glorious distance between two points.

"Rhythms of Grace"
by Carol Ward

3

Ars Poetica

A poem births anew like miracle
Words jigging loose,
juddering,
rushing full
Finding course
Words melodic and sizzling red
Words find their seat
but refuse to sit still

I am always searching
For the next sentence
I abandon one then pursue
The better sprawl

But oh the pleasure of
Pulling up shadow
To see the pouring forces beneath
That cresting tide

Oh poem I'll keep
Working on you until
You burst forth.

On Vacation

I'm on vacation
so today
I refuse to think about Race
And I refuse to think about my shining
almond skin
Or the ramifications of me saying
This as I do or that as I might
On white society

I'm on vacation so fuck it
I'm going to go sailing on a wide boat
And I'm not going to think about
This racist captain
Or the Middle Passage, I'm going to
Enjoy the whip of waves

I'm on vacation
I'm drinking wet-glassed mojitos on the beach
So I'm not going to think about
The Loiza oceans, and the enslaved
Brought to my mother's island and
I'll listen to the musica Africana
That keeps thrumming on my Mami's
Shores but it will be
Only sweet sound, normal noise

If you say hey Black girl, watch it negra
While I'm strolling on Condado,
I'm going to ignore the hell out of you.

Because today, while on vacation
I'm just me, in my new dress,
And my side-stepping walk, I'm chilling.
I'm not thinking strong.

Today I'm begging you
I'm on vacation,
I'll return to this dance on Monday,

So for now, just let me be.

Dark Woman

I inherited this Blackness
It is my treasured bright   blues
I wear it like old veil, I flaunt
It like church fan

I wear it like scattering blessing
My belonging: I carry it   I carry it   I   wield it
I   follow   it

            'Til the sun stops, watch:

You see it because I show it
I love it, oh I deeply love it
            (You act like I don't know
            it was once so terribly unloved)
Nothing you can do can bruise nor bludgeon it
My Blackness is never about you.

Voices

I am the voice hollering on the side corner
I am the voice whispering under the short jamb
I am the voice speaking slants to new companions
I am the voice talking mid-level at the podium

My voice drifts like sludge-slow river
My voice has a slicing edge
My voice is soft as little baby's fabric
My voice is raging like ripping flame

I claim all of my voices
They breathe and wriggle and press against me
Even if you don't understand
Why this smiling Black girl
Spits these heaving sentences

These voices tell me to fire on.

Love Songs for Oceans

Naples, Florida
I met you running from city spirits. I fled my Mami's Subaru, seeking you without knowing you in full. I drifted into your blue flesh when I was smaller and short-limbed. Your cobalts were a cure, you washed me, washed me. I let you pull me in close and I ruffled your rippling face. You were kind and sweet and true. After I left you, I thought of you every day, desperately.

Miami, Florida
You fizzled and flattened under fat purple cloud. You were stunning in your shine; I fit my board on your folds and you led me to your center, gently. You embraced me, lifted me told me new secrets and I knew you. I was certain I knew you.

Buye Beach, Puerto Rico
You are clear-skinned, poreless in your blue. I cut through you with my fingers and see my toes jigging at your swishing bottom. You are sky-colored, heated up and assured. You feel like my oldest home, I remember you from my mother's womb. A chorus of Boricuas croon balladas to you next to me and I let you overwhelm me, I sink down low. When I emerge from you, my curls flapping and wet, I hear a song ripping from Yemaya's lips. This is the first time I told you I loved you.

Carmel, California
You're soft and sure and your shore fluffs and fulls. You're widening until all I see is you and your stretching expanse. You are chilly to the touch but enveloping. When I tell you *I will only be here for a little while, I am leaving soon* you say *see you later, I'll beckon you again.*

Galveston, Texas
You are my home, now. I've never met an ocean like you. You are variously changing tone and temperature, most times you are dolphin-colored and you froth and foam blithely. You are confident in your brown-grey color and tell me to love my own skin. Your growing bubbles bless your shore. I wade into you and think, I can begin again, every day, with you.

"Rhythms of the Sea"
by Carol Ward

Naira Kuzmich

Sister-scribe,
You wrote me a letter,
asked me to pen a poem
for you if you didn't make it.

Lush-haired beauty with
a pearl-pure smile
you made the heart seize
and shudder when
you floated, body
queen-high
into the room

I am writing for you
dear Naira, red-lipped
and regal in
your glory

In another life,
we'd spend nights talking
about Toni and Gwendolyn
and the ones you love
and you would speak as you would
with mouth full of spirit
and scythe

The time we had was brief
but you knew my words
and saw straight through my skin
to find the brown flesh I try to conjure
on the page

In Everything I See Your Hand

And I see the work of your mouth
the sweep of your stretched fingers
the red blooms spilling
From your fire-fierce tongue

Dear Naira, sister-scribe
in everything, there
you are.

Carol Ward

You showed me your home,
Said I was always-invited and blessed to come

You never knew me when I was little and running
You never knew me when they shouted cusses at my name
You never knew me when I stood at the ledge and thought to tip

But you offered me your room and called
Me daughter
Oh woman, with paintbrush and weaving thread
You gave me your meals and told me I was yours

How can I forget your Godly kindness
How can I look past that warming love?
How can I see the world as you see it,
Kaleidoscopic, extraordinary, fringed with dream?

I talk to you normally but I see your length
You've told me of your mother-pains, I keep them close
You have transgressed the knife-sharp cliffs and valleys
And you are still here, asking
How are you today?

He told you I thought about dying
You prayed for me all night and the prayer worked
I am alive and I am breathing the new air
I am humming and happy and rolling in fields

Oh, Carol, I write you this poem
To let you know I will never know how
To return your love

But I will live this fresh life trying
I will always live in
Your hope

"Sea of Prayers"
by Carol Ward

Inevitable

Before the mirage, I see the zigzagging slap of sun
It's an easy light, rocking back and forth
Look, I see this as a simple art:

The bright on the summer porch rails, the moon
Hand-clamping the veranda

The night sky keeps talking about morning
I'm just a little child witnessing this all.

What to do when the sun is setting?
What to do when the inevitable comes?

I've spent my life counting time like pennies
In my Mami's cocina mason jar

But I know no matter what,
The next moment comes.

Publication Acknowledgements

"Past," "Aren't You Afraid," "Rooting," "Retribution," "Without Control." *Big Other: Puerto Rican Hauntology.* ed. John Madera.

"Because Tigers Will Never Change Their Stripes," "In Daddy's House." *Acentos Review.* ed. Jasminne Mendez.

"Apagón." *Entropy* & *Puerto Rico en mi corazon* ed. Roque Raquel Salas Rivera, Erica Mena, Richard Maldonado.

"Girl Candela," "Psalm 23," "Baggage," "Kinds of Grace." *Writing the Self-Elegy Anthology.* ed. Kara Dorris.

"Ancestry." *Journal of Western Folklore.*

"In the Meadow," "Worst Case Scenario," "Mental Health," "Night in Fort Pierce," and "Waiting." *Blacklandia: Black Experience Anthology.* ed. Romaine Washington

"Dark Woman," "Happy Day," "On Vacation." *La Libreta* ed. Peggy Robles-Alvarado

"Lost in Montjuïc, After Losing," "Descansar." *Zone 3.*

"Lying," "Voices." BIMBO: A Feminist Anthology, ed. Madison Whatley.

"Foremothers: Canonization, Recreation, Diaspora." *Obsidian.*

"Cálida." *Connotations Press.*

"Inevitable" "Diagnosis." *Afro-Hispanic Review.*

"Name." *West Trestle Review.*

Acknowledgements:

Mil gracias to Maritza González Cintrón and Carol Ward for your artwork.

Thank you to the cover artist Evie Shaffer and thank you to Edward Viduarre and Avery Castillo and everyone at FlowerSong for your investment in my poetry.

Thank you to my dear family and friends, all I do is for you.

About the Author

Jennifer Maritza McCauley is the author of the cross-genre collection *Scar On/Scar Off* which received an IPPY award and *When Trying to Return Home*, a short story collection, which was a New York Times Editors' Choice, called one of the Best Fiction Books of the Year according to Kirkus Reviews, a Must-Read of 2023 by Chicago Public Library and a Most Anticipated by Today. She received her MFA in creative writing from Florida International University and PhD in creative and literature from the University of Missouri-Columbia. She has been granted fellowships from the National Endowment for the Arts, Kimbilio and CantoMundo. She teaches at the University of Missouri-Kansas City (Fall '24) and is fiction editor at Pleiades.

FLOWERSONG
PRESS

FlowerSong Press nurtures essential verse from, about, and throughout the borderlands. Literary. Lyrical. Boundless.

Sign up for announcements about
new and upcoming titles at:

www.flowersongpress.com